The New Novello Choral Edition

ANTONIN DVOŘÁK
Te Deum

for soprano and bass soloists, SATB choir and orchestra

Vocal score

Revised by Michael Pilkington

Order No: NOV 078573

NOVELLO PUBLISHING LIMITED

It is requested that on all concert notices and programmes acknowledgement is made to 'The New Novello Choral Edition'.

Es wird gebeten, auf sämtlichen Konzertankündigungen und Programmen 'The New Novello Choral Edition' als Quelle zu erwähnen.

Il est exigé que toutes notices et programmes de concerts, comportent des remerciements à 'The New Novello Choral Edition'.

Orchestral material is available on hire from the Publisher.

Orchestermaterial ist beim Verlag erhältlich.

Les partitions d'orchestre sont en location disponibles chez l'editeur.

Permission to reproduce the Preface of this Edition must be obtained from the Publisher.

Die Erlaubnis, das Vorwort dieser Ausgabe oder Teile desselben zu reproduzieren, muß beim Verlag eingeholt werden.

Le droit de reproduction de ce document à partir de la préface doit être obtenu de l'éditeur.

© 2003 Novello & Company Limited

Published in Great Britain by Novelle Publishing Limited
Head Office: 14-15 Berners Street, London W1T 3LJ
Tel +44 (0)20 7434 0066   Fax +44 (0)20 7287 6329

Sales and Hire: Music Sales Distribution Centre
Newmarket Road, Bury St Edmunds, Suffolk, IP33 3YB
Tel +44 (0)1284 702600   Fax +44 (0)1284 768301

www.musicroom.com   e-mail: music@musicsales.co.uk

All rights reserved   Printed in Great Britain

Music setting by Barnes Music Engraving Limited

PREFACE

In the autumn of 1892, Dvořák was to take up the post of Director of the National Conservatory in New York. In June of that year, Jeanette Thurber, founder of the National Conservatory, asked him to write a festive cantata, for which she would send him a text. This was to celebrate the quartercentenary of Columbus's discovery of America. There being no sign of the promised text, however, Dvořák decided to set the Te Deum for the occasion. Though the work is divided into four sections it was originally designed to be performed without breaks. The composer's family own the original sketches of the work, and also the autograph full score. However, the fair copy prepared for the publisher is no longer extant, and it is clear from the first edition, published by Simrock in 1896, that Dvořák had, as was his habit, revised the work considerably before publication. The editors of the Critical Edition (Supraphon 1969) therefore consider 'the only truly valid source for a new edition of the work...is Simrock's edition. A comparison of this with the autograph ... served for the amendment of a few oversights in the printed edition'. In fact the editors have made a large number of changes and additions to slurs and articulations throughout the work, in the interests of consistency, few of which are commented on in their critical notes. The present edition is based firmly on Simrock. It is very clear that Dvořák was in the habit of varying the articulation of his themes at each appearance. For example, in bar 3 of the first movement note 6 in the violins has a stress accent in Simrock and the last 2 notes in the bar have staccato dots and a slur, the same point in bar 11 has a mordent at note 6 and nothing for the last two notes. The Complete Works editors have changed note 6 in bar 3 to a mordent, citing bar 11; the end of the bar, however, is left without adjustment. In the middle section of this movement, bars 56-109, there are short decorative passages for flute and clarinet, or flute and cor anglais; the phrasing in Simrock is different for each appearance, but has been 'corrected' without comment in the Complete Works. I have provided a new piano reduction for this edition.

Sources, as given in the Complete Works edition:

A   Autograph of the full score.

S   Simrock full score 1896.

ES   Supraphon full score 1969.

Notes.

1   Bar 121: **S** is inconsistent in the markings for violins and viola. Violin 1 has staccato dots for notes 2-8; violin 2 has accents for notes 2-4, but nothing for notes 5-8; viola has no markings. **ES** gives accents for all three parts for notes 2-8 without comment, but considering the woodwind, perhaps the staccato of violin 1 is correct and the accents in violin 2 here in error.

3   Bar 11: the dynamics seem strange. The bass soloist has *mf* in **S** and *f* in **A**, followed by **ES**; *mf* matches the doubling horn melody, but as the accompanying woodwind are *f*, should not the tune be *f* and the accompaniment *mf*, or more probably all parts *f* as in the surrounding appearances of the theme?

4   Bar 22: violin note 2 is given as d″ natural in all sources, contradicting the d′♯ in the viola; since the remainder of the phrase has violin 1 doubling the voice, f″♯ seems certainly correct.
    Bar 79: flutes 2 last note is b″ in **S**, but e‴ in **A**, followed by **ES**; this matches violin 2, but comparison with bar 119 of the first movement suggests the possibility that the violin was in error rather than the flute.

Michael Pilkington
Old Coulsdon

TE DEUM

Antonín Dvořák, Op. 103

Coro No. 1

Pa - - trem om - nis ter - - - ra__ ve - ne -
ter - - ra, om - nis ter - - - ra ve - ne -
ve - ne - ra - tur, om - nis ter - - - ra ve - ne -
ter - - ra, om - nis ter - ra ve - ne - ra - - tur, ve - ne -

- ra - tur.
- ra - tur.   Te
- ra - tur.   Te
- ra - tur.   Te

Te æ - ter - num Pa - - - trem om - nis ter - ra

om - nis ter - ra, om - nis ter - ra

om - nis ter - ra ve - ne - ra - tur, om - nis_ ter - ra__

om - - nis ter - ra, om - nis_ ter - ra__

ve - ne - ra - - - tur.

ve - ne - ra - - tur.

ve - ne - ra - - - tur.

ve - ne - ra - - tur.

D **Un poco meno mosso** ♩ = 76

SOPRANO SOLO
[m.v.]

San - ctus, san - ctus, san - ctus Do - mi-nus De - us Sa - ba-oth.

pp *pp*

Ple - ni sunt cæ - li, cæ - li et ter - ra ma-je - sta - tis glo - ri-æ

f *p* > *pp*

cresc. *mf* *fz* *p* > *pp*

E *p*

tu - æ. Te glo - ri -

p *pp* *pp legato*

Chorus

-o - - sus_ A-po-sto-lo-rum cho - rus.

TENOR: San - ctus Do - mi-nus De - us

BASS: San - ctus Do - mi-nus De - us

Te Pro-phe - ta - - rum lau-da - bi-lis nu - me-rus.

Sa - ba - oth._____

Sa - ba - oth._____

Te per or-bem ter-ra - rum san-cta con-fi-te - tur Ec-

Sa - ba-oth._____

Sa - ba-oth._____

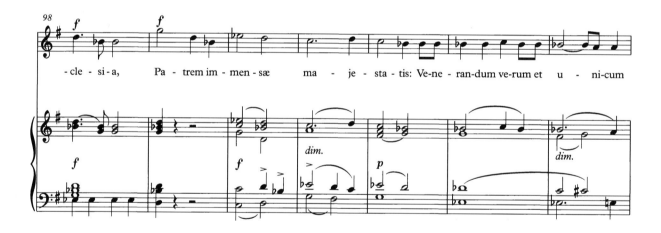

-cle - si - a, Pa - trem im - men-sæ ma - je - sta-tis: Ve-ne - ran-dum ve-rum et u - ni-cum

Fi - lium: Sanc-tum quo-que Pa - ra-cle-tum Spi - ri - tum._____

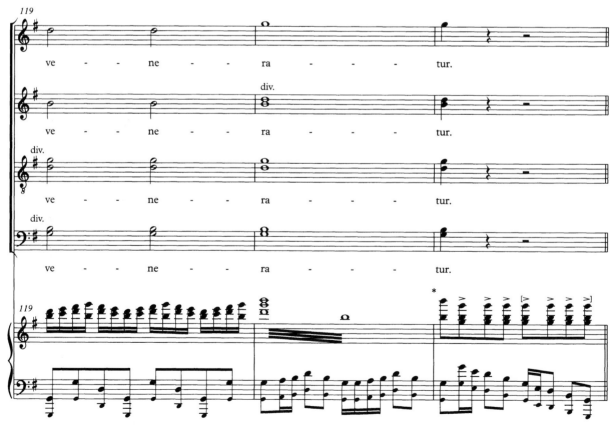

attacca

* see Preface

Coro No. 2

Tu Pa - tris sem - pi-ter - nus,

Tu Pa - tris es Fi - li - us.

Tu_____ ad li - be - ran - - dum sus - ce - ptu - rus

* RH: last 3 c's ♮, **S**.

ho - mi - nem, non hor - ru -

- i - sti Vir - gi - nis u - te -

- rum. Tu, de - vic - to mor - tis a - cu - le-o,

a - pe - ru - i - sti cre - den - ti - bus re - gna

L Tempo I Meno mosso ♩ = 60

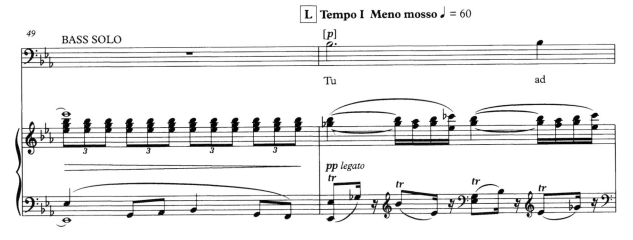

BASS SOLO

[*p*]

Tu ad

dex - - te - ram De - i

se - - - des in

glo - - ria Pa - tris, in

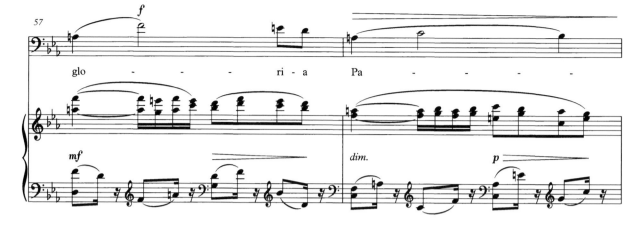

* Tenor note 1: flat missing **ES**

[attacca]

Coro No. 3

* see Preface

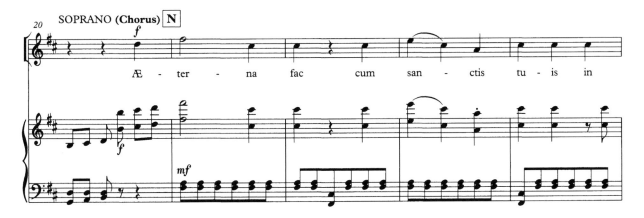

29

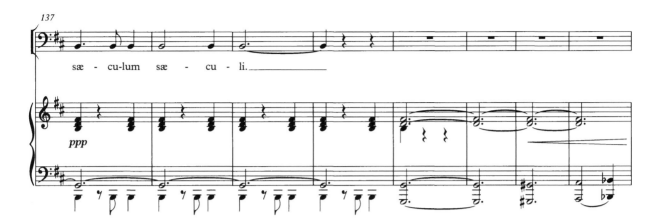

sæ - cu-lum sæ - cu - li.

ppp

molto espressivo

ffz — — f fz dim.

S

p pp

ppp pp

[attacca]

Coro No. 4

* Soprano note 4: no gracenote in **S**, present in **A**, **ES**

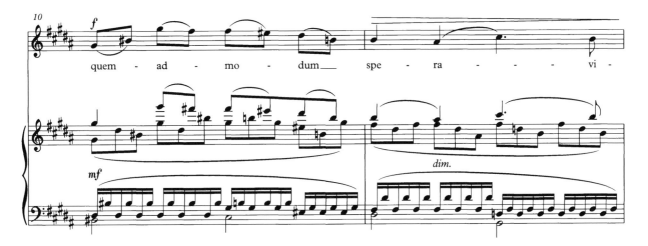

quem - ad - mo - dum___ spe - ra - - - vi -

- mus in___ te.___

Poco meno mosso
Chorus
TENOR

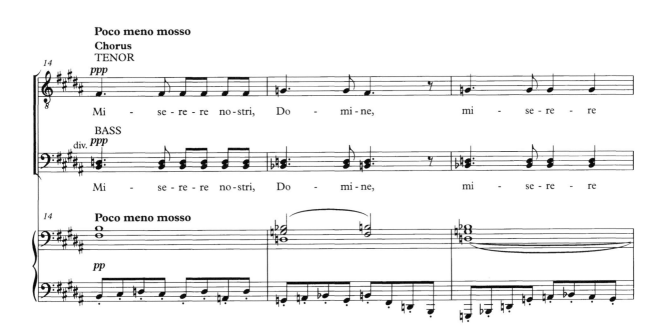

Mi - se - re - re no-stri, Do - mi - ne, mi - se - re - re

BASS

Mi - se - re - re no-stri, Do - mi - ne, mi - se - re - re

Poco meno mosso

* RH upper note 2: d' natural (!), **S**, **ES**, see Preface.

In te, Do - mi-ne, spe - ra - vi:

non con - fun - dar, non con - fun - dar

in æ - ter - num.

Chorus
TENOR

Mi - se -

BASS

Mi - se -

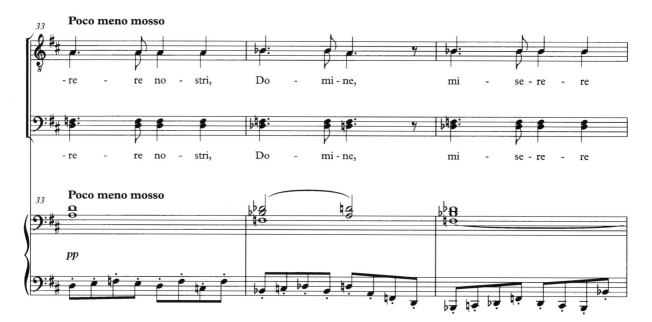

re - re no - stri, Do - mi - ne, mi - se - re - re

re - re no - stri, Do - mi - ne, mi - se - re - re

SOPRANO SOLO

Be - ne - di - ca - mus

BASS SOLO

Be - ne - di - ca - mus

no - stri.

no - stri.

* see Preface

NOVELLO REVISED STANDARD CHORAL EDITIONS

Fully revised and edited performing versions of many of the major works in the large-scale choral concert repertoire, replacing the standard Novello editions, often putting back the composers' intentions, restoring the original text, modernised accompaniments and providing new English translations.
Orchestral material, where necessary, is available on hire.

J.S. BACH
(ed. Neil Jenkins)
Christmas Oratorio
NOV072500
German and English text
Magnificats in D & E♭
NOV072529
German and English text in the four Lauds in the E♭ version
Mass in B minor NOV078430
St. John Passion
NOV072489
German and English text
St. Matthew Passion
NOV072478
German and English text

BEETHOVEN
(ed. Michael Pilkington)
Choral Finale to the Ninth Symphony
NOV072490
German and English text
Mass in C
NOV078560
Missa Solemnis (Mass in D)
NOV072497

BRAHMS
(Pilkington)
A German Requiem
NOV072492
German and English text

DVOŘÁK
(Pilkington)
Mass in D NOV072491
Requiem NOV072516
Stabat Mater NOV072503
Te Deum NOV078573

ELGAR
(ed. Bruce Wood)
The Dream of Gerontius
NOV072530
Great Is the Lord
NOV078595

GOUNOD
(Pilkington)
Messe solennelle de Sainte Cécile
NOV072495

HANDEL
Belshazzar
(ed. Donald Burrows) NOV070530
Four Coronation Anthems
NOV072507
  The King Shall Rejoice
  (ed. Damian Cranmer)
  Let Thy Hand be Strengthened
  (Burrows)
  My Heart is Inditing *(Burrows)*
  Zadok the Priest *(Burrows)*
Judas Maccabaeus
(ed. Merlin Channon)
NOV072486
The King Shall Rejoice
(Cranmer) NOV072496
Messiah
(ed. Watkins Shaw) NOV070137
  Study Score NOV890031
**O Praise the Lord
(from Chandos Anthem No. 9)**
(ed. Graydon Beeks) NOV072511
This Is the Day
(ed. Burrows) NOV072510
Zadok the Priest
(Burrows) NOV290704

HAYDN
(ed. Pilkington)
The Creation
NOV072485
German and English text
The Seasons
NOV072493
German and English text
Te Deum Laudamus
NOV078463
"Maria Theresa" Mass
NOV078474
Mass "In Time of War"
NOV072514
"Nelson" Mass
NOV072513
Harmoniemesse
NOV078507

MAUNDER
Olivet to Calvary
NOV072487

MENDELSSOHN
(Pilkington)
Elijah
NOV070201
German and English text

Hymn of Praise
NOV072506

MOZART
Requiem
(ed. Duncan Druce) NOV070529
**Coronation Mass
(Mass in C K.317)**
(Pilkington) NOV072505
Mass in C minor
(reconstr. Philip Wilby) NOV078452

PURCELL
Come, Ye Sons of Art, Away
(Wood) NOV072467
Welcome to All the Pleasures
(Wood) NOV290674
Ed. Vol. 15 Royal Welcome Songs 1
(Wood) NOV151102
Ed. Vol. 22A Catches
(ed. Ian Spink) NOV151103

ROSSINI
(Pilkington)
Petite messe solennelle
NOV072436

SCHUBERT
Mass in G, D.167 (SSA version)
NOV070258

SCHÜTZ
(Jenkins)
Christmas Story
NOV072525
German and English text

STAINER
(ed. Pilkington)
The Crucifixion
NOV072488

VERDI
(Pilkington)
Requiem
NOV072403

VIVALDI
(ed. Jasmin Cameron)
Gloria
NOV078441